Exploring the Genesis Creation and Fall Stories

John Michael Perry

Sheed & Ward

Other titles in this series:

- Exploring the Transfiguration Story
- Exploring the Resurrection of Jesus
- Exploring the Origins and Evolution of Eucharist in the New Testament

---

Sheed & Ward™ is a service of National Catholic Reporter Publishing Company, Inc.

Library of Congress Cataloguing-in-Publication Data

Perry, John M., 1929-
  Exploring the Genesis creation and fall stories / John Michael Perry.
        p.   cm.
    ISBN 1-55612-553-4 (alk. paper)
    1. Bible. O.T. Genesis I-III—Criticism, interpretation, etc. I. Title.
  BS1235.2.P47   1992   92-5024
  222'.1106--dc20   CIP

Published by: Sheed & Ward
                 115 E. Armour Blvd. P.O. Box 419492
                 Kansas City, MO 64141-6492

To order, call: (800) 333-7373

Contents

Part One: Introduction

1.

IT IS ALMOST IMPOSSIBLE TO EXAGGERATE the importance that the story of humankind's creation and fall plays in the mental life of people who participate in Western culture. What we think about humankind's beginning has a profound impact on our present self-understanding and sense of destiny. Even when we are not consciously reflecting on the creation paradigm learned from our cultural tradition, it exercises unconscious influence on our general awareness of the meaning of our existence. It is fitting, therefore, to spend time deepening our insight into the venerable creation and fall stories which we find in the book of Genesis. After we have reviewed the historical circumstances and special religious concerns that contributed to the formation of these inspired accounts, we will examine their relevance for our age.

The reader should be aware from the outset that the approach to the creation and fall stories presented herein is that of modern biblical criticism. This approach assumes that God did not dictate the Genesis creation and fall accounts to their authors. Rather, he inspired these authors to use traditions already known to them, and to creatively expand such traditions with religious ideas of their own.

It follows, therefore, that the stories we will be considering are not literal accounts which derive from an eyewitness. Instead, they are the inspired imaginings of human beings who lived at varying times and places in the Ancient Near East; these storytellers were encouraged by their experience of God to advance the great dialog in human history concerning the origin of our world and the troubling presence therein of sin, suffering, and death.

2.

CONTEMPORARY BIBLICAL SCHOLARSHIP tells us that there are actually two creation stories (and indications of a third) in the first three chapters of Genesis. These stories were gradually created, revised, and combined during the course of many centuries, and their ancient authors left witting and unwitting clues which enable us to arrive at a number of fascinating insights into the circumstances that led to their formation. We shall discuss the most important of these clues as we proceed.

The more ancient of the two creation accounts is attributed to an author who is called "the Yahwist" because he almost always gives God the name "Yahweh" when telling the story of creation. "Yahweh" is the personal name for God that the ancient Israelites believed God had revealed to them through Moses; its disclosure is related in Exodus 3:13-15.

The more recent of the ancient creation stories is attributed to a man called "the Priestly Author." Although it is highly probable that both of these ancient authors were priests, the one who wrote later is expressly so designated because he belonged to the group of priestly writers who acted as the final editors of the law of Moses during and shortly after the Exile to Babylon (c. 587-500 B.C.). His viewpoint, and that of his colleagues, is consistently characterized by "priestly" concerns of a legal-liturgical kind. While recounting the work of creation, the Priestly Author always refers to the Creator as "God" and never uses the personal name that God revealed to Moses. He refrains from doing so because shortly after the exile the Jewish priests began teaching their people that, out of reverence, they should avoid using God's personal name.

The first biblical scholar in history to call "critical" attention to the discrepant way God is named in the creation stories was a Flemish Jesuit, Cornelius a Lapide. He taught scripture in Rome from 1616 to 1636 A.D., and observed that two creation accounts should be distinguished in Genesis because God is signified differently in one (1:1-2:4a) as compared to the other (2:4b-3:24). He suggested (mistakenly but seminally) that Moses must have known and included an older creation story along with his own inspired account.

A Lapide's view was understandably alarming to almost everyone concerned with the Bible in his day. Ancient Jewish and Christian tradition had long assumed that Moses wrote all the material in the five books attributed to him—Genesis, Exodus, Leviticus, Numbers, and Deuteronomy. This tradition arose because the folk mentality which characterized the ancient Israelites led them to attribute all later additions to the law of Moses to Moses himself.

The priests of ancient Israel thought of themselves as disciples of Moses entrusted with the tasks of explaining and developing his sacred law for later generations. By associating necessary additions to the law with its original bestowal by God through Moses, the priests intended to guarantee the sacred authority of such additions and thereby motivate the Israelites to observe them.

The overwhelming majority of a Lapide's contemporaries lacked the specialized knowledge needed to understand his conclusion; as a result, the Holy Roman Inquisition compelled him to renounce it under pain of death. He did so publicly, but privately remained convinced that his positing of two distinct creation stories was correct and would someday be vindicated. Biblical scholars in the eighteenth and nineteenth centuries rediscovered the valid substance of a Lapide's insight, and it is now generally accepted in qualified form.

In addition to discrepant ways of naming God, there are other striking differences in the creation stories written by the Yahwist and the Priestly Author. The Yahwist says that God created everything in *one* day (2:4b), formed the man *first* (2:7), then the animals (2:19), and *finally* the woman (2:22). After he relates the creation of the man and his wife, the Yahwist continues with the story of their fall from God's favor, and the origin of sin, suffering, and death in our world. Throughout his account, the Yahwist describes God's activity in a grossly anthropomorphic way (i.e., interpreting the nonhuman in human terms), and does not hesitate to have God make personal appearances and speak directly to other participants in the story (3:8-19).

Conversely, the Priestly Author describes God's creative activity as spread over *six* days (1:31-2:1), and emphasizes that God *rested* on the seventh day (2:2-3). We shall learn below that he was inspired to write his account while in Babylon, very early in the postexilic period, to encourage observance of the Sabbath *rest*. Gross anthropomorphism is avoided by the Priestly author; God never appears in his account; we only *hear* God's creative commands being spoken with transcendent majesty. And the Priestly author tells us that God created both of the humans *last*, on the sixth day (1:26-27, 31). He makes no mention of their fall from divine favor, although he does make an unusual allusion to the aftermath of their fall in 1:26, which will be explained later.

Even though the Priestly Author wrote his account around 450 years after that of the Yahwist, his account appears first. This is so because the Priestly Author was one of the final editors of the Pentateuch (the first five books of the Bible), and was free to arrange things as he saw fit. We shall see below that he wrote his new creation account to deal with a serious pastoral problem. In his judgment, the problem was so critical that it justified placing his new account in front of the old one as a solemn introduction.

We will now turn to a more detailed examination of the two creation stories and consider the historical and religious background that influenced their form and content. While there is a wealth of interesting and important things that could be said about each of the creation stories, we will limit our attention to ideas deemed more beneficial for the nonspecialist. Since the Yahwist wrote the earliest of the two accounts, we will begin with him. From this point forward, the reader is urged to open his or her Bible and relate the explanation being provided to the indicated text. This will become especially important when we begin to analyze the creation and fall accounts themselves. Readers who ignore this advice will fail to fully grasp much of what is being explained.

Questions for Further Study

1. In what basic and important way does the modern approach to understanding the Genesis creation and fall stories differ from the traditional approach?

2. Who was the first Christian biblical scholar to teach that there are distinguishable creation stories in Genesis which name God in different ways? When and where did he teach?

3. Why do religious ideas that are eventually accepted as true frequently meet with opposition when they first appear?

4. Aside from the different ways in which they name God, what other major differences distinguish the Yahwist's creation and fall story from the Priestly Author's account?

Part Two: The Yahwist's Account

1.

THE YAHWIST probably wrote his account c. 950 B.C. during the reign of King Solomon. This judgment is based on a number of indications found in the account itself. These indications, some obvious, some subtle, will be discussed later. The reader must finally judge whether or not the interpretation based on them seems probable.

We know it was only after an uncertain beginning (1 Kgs. 1:1-53) that Solomon consolidated his right to rule over the imperial kingdom established by David, his father. There are indications that once his claim to the throne was firmly secured, he asked the priests in Jerusalem to put in writing the sacred history of Israel, most of which had been preserved orally for centuries. By commissioning such a history for his royal archives, Solomon was following long established royal practice in the Ancient Near East. But more importantly, he probably wanted God's promise to David of a *permanent* dynasty (2 Sam. 7:12-16) and his own anointing in David's lifetime as David's *successor* (1 Kgs. 1:1-48) to receive pride of place in this history.

Solomon knew that his right to rule as a Davidite over all of Israel was disputed by some among the northern tribes (2 Sam. 20:1-22), and also that his older brother Adonijah, encouraged by custom and powerful allies, contested Solomon's right to be David's successor (1 Kgs. 1:5-53). It was to Solomon's advantage, therefore, to have a history of the nation *and* the monarchy written by the Jerusalem priests who supported the Davidic dynasty and David's choice of Solomon as his successor (1 Kgs. 1:32-39).

The evidence suggests that a number of priests probably collaborated in carrying out Solomon's commission, each authoring or editing an assigned part of the requested history. Such collaboration is inferred from the remarkable number of historical works that appeared during the reign of Solomon, each dealing with a segment of Israel's history from the period of the patriarchs up to and including the reign of Solomon. These works are unified by a common conviction that the dynasty of David is of central importance in God's saving purpose for Israel and the nations, and that Solomon is David's divinely favored heir.

In defense of that conviction, these priest-historians share various foreshadowing techniques and theological motifs which they probably agreed upon and strategically located within their respective portions of the history. The priest-historian who particularly concerns us is the one who wrote down and interpreted the earliest traditions of Israel that deal with the patriarchs, the sojourn in Egypt, the exodus, the covenant at Sinai, and the forty year sojourn in the desert; it is this priest who is called the Yahwist.

In league with the other priest-historians mentioned above, the Yahwist alludes to the dynasty of David as divinely foreintended (Gen. 49:8-12; Num. 24:7, 9, 17), and shares their conviction that God sovereignly rejects human expectations by electing the *younger* son (Shem,

Isaac, Judah, Epharaim, Jacob, Perez, David, Solomon)
rather than the *older* son (Cain, Ishmael, Reuben,
Manasseh, Esau, Zerah, Eliab, Adonijah), thereby lending
divine sanction to the replacement of the "older" dynasty
of Saul by the "younger" dynasty of David, and especially
to Solomon's superseding his older brother Adonijah in
their struggle for David's throne. Since the Yahwist so
evidently pursued a program of justifying the dynasty of
David and the succession of Solomon, it is inconceivable
that he would have concluded his work without recounting the history of both men unless he knew that one of his
priestly collaborators intended to do so.

In addition to legitimizing the dynasty of David and
succession of Solomon, the Yahwist and his collaborators
consistently weave the theme of sin and punishment into
their work. They tirelessly reiterate that the significant
persons in salvation history who *obey* God are blessed,
while all those who *disobey* are punished. The Yahwist
and his colleagues were manifestly trying to encourage
King Solomon to faithfully obey Yahweh, and to warn him
against the folly of failing to do so. We shall be reminded
below that they had good reason to be preoccupied with
Solomon's conduct.

Priestly collaboration in pursuit of shared theological
aims is also indicated by the carefully orchestrated way in
which unusual language found in the history of the Yahwist (e.g., "good and evil," Gen. 2:17; 3:5,22; "seed," Gen.
3:15) is repeated in the work of his colleagues (2 Sam.
14:17; 7:l2; 1 Kgs. 3:9).

In the judgment of the Yahwist and his priestly confreres, it was through the everlasting dynasty promised to
David (2 Sam. 7:13-15; 23:5) that God had begun to re-
store his kingly rule over the kingdom of creation disrupted by the disobedience of Adam. It was imperative,
therefore, to impress upon King Solomon his sacred duty,
as the earthly representative of God's kingly reign, to use

his reputed "wisdom" to judge rightly between "good and evil," which the original king of creation had foolishly failed to do (Gen. 2:17; 3:5-6, 22). To achieve their aim, several allusions to the king's obligation to discern sagaciously between "good and evil" were made at appropriate places in the histories of David (2 Sam. 14:17) and Solomon (1 Kgs. 3:9). The related use of the term "seed" will be explained later.

2.

FULFILLING SOLOMON'S COMMISSION provided the Yahwist an opportunity to deal with an especially pressing concern of his own. We have good reason to think he and the other priests in Jerusalem were deeply troubled by Solomon's religious concessions to his foreign wives. Solomon had taken into his harem numerous daughters of foreign kings. These royal wives were allowed to maintain allegiance to the gods of their own nations and even prevailed upon Solomon to build shrines just outside Jerusalem where they could worship them:

> Then Solomon built a high place for Chemosh the abomination of Moab, and for Molech the abomination of the Ammonites, on the mountain east of Jerusalem. And so he did for all his foreign wives, who burned incense and sacrificed to their gods. And the Lord was angry with Solomon, because his heart had turned away from the Lord, the God of Israel. . . . (1 Kgs 11:7-9)

Solomon doubtlessly considered his compliance with the wishes of his foreign wives as nothing more than political expedience, but in the eyes of the priests of Yahweh in Jerusalem, he was in alarming violation of the first and most important of the ten commandments enshrined in the ark of the covenant, and was inviting upon himself and the nation the wrath of Yahweh, who throned upon the ark.

The Yahwist and his priestly confreres knew full well that it would be dangerous to directly challenge the policies of the king. Within living memory, King Saul had brutally executed Ahimelech, and all the other priests at Nob, because he mistakenly suspected them of treasonous complicity with David (1 Sam 22:11-19). Consequently, the Yahwist, probably in consultation with his priestly colleagues, chose to provide Solomon with a *veiled* warning, prudently indirect, but still able to admonish Solomon concerning his folly.

To achieve his goal, the Yahwist conceived an ingenious plan: he prefaced the earliest portion of the history requested by Solomon with a history of creation and the origin and spread of sin among the nations. For his introduction, he revised an ancient myth already known to Israel, which recounted the creation and tragic *fall* of the first man, who was *king* over creation. By such a tactic, the Yahwist hoped to make Solomon aware of the potentially destructive consequences of his behavior.

3.

THE READER SHOULD BE FOREWARNED that the text of the Yahwist's creation and fall account is the product of a complex history. Four distinct stages in that history must be distinguished. At the *first* stage, the account was created by a polytheistic mythmaker in southern Mesopotamia, in either oral or written form. At the *second* stage, the account was brought from Mesopotamia to the land of Canaan and translated into Hebrew, a Canaanite dialect. At the *third* stage, most of the account's explicit polytheistic references were removed by the Israelites to make it compatible with the demands of their covenant God for exclusive worship. At the *fourth* stage, the Yahwist rearranged, revised, and expanded parts of the account to prompt a change in Solomon's behavior. The reasons for positing these four stages will become apparent as we proceed.

Various clues in the traditional creation myth revised by by the Yahwist indicate that its original form was forged in the mental fires of a Mesopotamian mythmaker long before Israel became a nation; it was possibly mediated to Israel through her patriarchal ancestors who had emigrated from Mesopotamia to the land of Canaan, but it is also possible that the story was known to the Canaanites, and Israel learned it from them. The story related that the first man was tempted to disobey God; he foolishly did so and lost the right, for himself and all other humans, to eat the fruit of the tree of life (the continued eating of which conferred immortality).

In the traditional story which antedated the Yahwist's revision, the woman was not created until *after* the man's fall and expulsion from the garden and, therefore, played no role in his temptation. That is why she is absent in the *unedited* passages from the earlier version where God (1) warns *only* the man about the deadly consequences of eating the forbidden fruit (2:16-17), (2) rebukes *only* the man for disobeying (3:22-23), and (3) drives him *alone* from the garden (3:24). These three passages differ noticeably from the material later placed between them by the Yahwist; there the man and his wife are always mentioned *together* when both are involved in the unfolding action (2:21-24; 3:6-21).

Postulating the woman's later insertion into the temptation scene helps explain how she knows about the prohibition against eating the forbidden fruit (3:2-3) even though she was not informed thereof by God or her husband in the narrative which precedes her creation. Her knowledge derives not from God or her husband, but from the Yahwist, who, in anxious pursuit of his purpose, neglected her instruction.

The Yahwist decided to change the original story so that the man is tempted to disobey God not by the serpent, but by the coaxing of his wife (3:6b), thereby providing Solomon with a striking parallel to what was currently happening between himself and his foreign wives. To achieve this end, the Yahwist moved the creation of the man's wife from after to before the fall (2:18-24) so that she can be the one who succumbs to the serpent's temptation (3:1-6a), and becomes, in turn, the one who directly tempts her husband to disobey God (3:6b). We will return to the Yahwist's faith-inspired restructuring of Israel's traditional creation myth after a brief and important digression.

4.

SINCE THE WORD 'MYTH' still has a bad reputation in some circles, it seems appropriate to briefly mention its creative function at the precritical stage of human thinking, the stage dominated by picture language, the logic of unconscious associations, and a naive reading of causality. Before the ancient Greeks introduced philosophical reasoning, myth was the only form of creative interpretation available to humans. A myth is a story which provides a precritical answer to some question. The Yahwistic creation myth known to ancient Israel was meant to explain the origin of humans and the disruptive presence of sin, suffering, and death in their world.

It is true that myth is naive in some respects, for it has not yet learned to distinguish between invisible *natural* forces and *ultimate* causal power. Myth, however, correctly discerns that the law of causality which is operating everywhere in the universe must be invoked to explain the invisible causes of visible effects. This fundamentally correct insight later evolves into abstract philosophical reasoning and is the remote ancestor of scientific hypothesizing.

To correctly grasp the meaning of a myth, we must: (1) understand that it uses *symbolic analogy,* i.e., it illustrates obscurely known things by *comparing* them to clearly known things that are judged to be similar; (2) recognize that the symbolic comparisons being made are based on conscious or unconscious *associations*; (3) be guided by the associations to a recognition of the *question* for which the myth is a precritical *answer*; and, (4) remember that the myth's interpretation of causality is naive.

For example, the oldest of the two Genesis creation stories states that God shaped the first human out of clay (2:7). The Mesopotamian mythmaker who initiated this statement intended it to answer the question of our ultimate origin. Neither he nor the Yahwist who later concurred with this part of his account had any specific information about human origins, yet their knowledge of cause and effect told them that there must have been an originating Cause or Creator who somehow produced the first human.

To illustrate this insight, the mythmaker chose an example of creative activity familiar to his society, that of an artisan shaping an image of a human out of clay. The explanation provided by this comparison failed to realize that God created humans *indirectly* through the evolutionary process, but it correctly understood that God is the ultimate Cause of humankind.

Because we humans are self-transcending beings who can think (with mathematical infinity) about transcending all limits, it is inevitable that we aspire to unending life and are profoundly troubled by the limiting experience of death. Most of us have been convinced intuitively by the implications of our extraordinary design that we are destined for immortality, and that death will not be the end of our story. That is why we are the only species that buries its dead (and in past ages, provided them with items deemed necessary for future life).

Our ability to think about transcending death suggests, but does not prove, that we are already empowered to transcend it. Likewise, because of our astonishing ability to think about infinity, eternity, and immortality, we infer with good reason that we were designed to participate, in some wonderful and mysterious way, in the infinity and eternity of our ultimate Source. And yet, when we consider the ambiguous nature of death in the light of our burden of personal guilt, we experience anxious uncertainty: will death bring positive transformation, or punishment in some unending form?

The Mesopotamian mythmaker who provided the original form of ancient Israel's creation and fall story shared our humanity, our aspiration to immortality, and our uncertainty about tragedy, guilt, suffering, and death. He was aware, long before the existentialist philosophers, that we finite human beings are inescapably threatened by nonbeing as we journey anxiously through time. The creation myth he composed was an ancient attempt to answer the perennial questions raised by our problematic existence. Since death is the most serious punishment that humans can inflict on one another, and all humans have had to suffer and die from the time of their beginning, the mythmaker (and the Yahwist) presumed that God must be punishing humankind collectively for some serious offense committed by our first parents.

Both the Mesopotamian mythmaker and the Yahwist correctly realized that humans are destined by design for immortality. Their mistake lay in assuming that we were intended by our Creator to receive immortality at the *beginning* of our physical existence instead of its *conclusion*. Accordingly, the answer they assigned to the question of death was decidedly pessimistic, for they were not privileged to know the Risen Jesus and the gift of the Spirit mediated through him as God's definitive answer to our ultimate questions. At their time and place in history, death seemed like permanent punishment for sin. It was not until the arrival of apocalyptic theology in the book of Daniel, eight centuries later, c. 165 B.C., that ancient Israel began to hope that the immortality which Adam lost for humankind at the beginning could be regained at the end (Dan. 12:2-3,9).

5.

THE TRADITIONAL CREATION STORY which the Yahwist found ready to revise, begins by describing the earth as a barren steppe on which God has not yet caused rain to fall (2:4b-5). A stream welling up from beneath the earth's surface is the only source of water (2:6). We are told that God had not sent rain because there was no "man" to till the ground (2:5). The Hebrew word in the story customarily translated as "man" really means "human," but the accompanying personal pronouns make clear that the human is male. There is obvious wordplay in the Hebrew text between the word for the human (adam) and that for the ground (adamah) from which he was formed (2:7).

Several of the details in the story's introductory verses suggest its place of origin. To begin with, the primeval earth has been given the characteristics of southern Mesopotamia's parched alluvial plain, where insufficient rainfall required farmers to carefully irrigate their crops with water drawn from a nearby river or canal. Accordingly, God is described as a wise landowner who does not waste water unless there is a human to use it in tilling the soil (2:5).

The story assumes that the occupation of the earliest humans was farming rather than hunting and gathering. At the time when the story was created, humans had been farming in Mesopotamia for so many millennia that they could no longer remember an age when there had been no farmers. (That humans were farmers from their very beginning is also presupposed in the Babylonian creation myth, the Enuma elish, which states that humans had been created to grow food for the gods and provide their sustenance.) We are next told that God, acting as a divine artisan, made the first man out of clay (2:7); this again suggests Mesopotamia where almost everything was made of clay because stands of timber and quarry stone were lacking. In Mesopotamia, not only were temples and palaces made of clay bricks, but even letters were inscribed on clay and delivered in baked clay envelopes. In a society where artisans ordinarily made everything of clay, a storyteller would not hesitate to describe a *divine* artisan forming the first human (and later, the animals, 2:19) from clay. Significantly, the Babylonian creation myth also says that the god Marduk made humans from "clay" mixed with the blood of Kingu, a god whom Marduk had slain.

6.

WE MUST NOW DIRECT OUR ATTENTION to an important linguistic problem in the Yahwist's creation myth. The explanation which follows will be a bit technical, but is *essential* to our purpose. The reader who finds it tedious is encouraged to persevere.

The Hebrew word in the creation stories usually translated as "God" is really a plural noun (*elohim*) which means "gods" or "heavenly beings" (the singular form is *el*). This plural noun for deity (along with the plural pronoun in 3:22: "Behold, the man has become like one of us. . . .") suggests that the Mesopotamian author who originally conceived the story was a polytheist who spoke of creation as the work of the "gods" acting in concert. The plural noun for deity was probably retained when the earlier account was translated into Hebrew, either by Israel's Hebrew-speaking ancestors (who had emigrated to Canaan) or the Canaanites (Hebrew is a

Canaanite dialect). By the time the Israelites who came after Moses inherited the story, they had become devoted *henotheists*, i.e., they worshiped their national God to the jealous *exclusion* of foreign gods, who were still thought to exist (Exod. 20:3; Pss. 89:5-8; 95:3). At some stage in their divinely encouraged adjustment to the monotheizing logic implicit in henotheism, they decided that their covenant God, Yahweh, had created the world without the involvement of other gods.

After this critical transition, the Israelites enigmatically retained the *plural* word "gods" (*elohim*) in their creation story, but now understood it as *singular* in meaning and referring only to their God; at this stage the priest-reciters of the story would have changed its plural pronouns for deity to singular forms (with the intriguing exception of 3:22).

The historical and linguistic evidence indicates that when the ancestors of Israel arrived in the land of Canaan and learned Hebrew, they also learned that the god El reigned supreme over the Canaanite pantheon and they began identifying the God of their fathers with this god. The inclusion of the divine name El in the names of Israelites occurred frequently in early Isra-el, and from the Mosaic period (when Moses introduced God's personal name) till the monarchy, the names El and Yahweh were both in use. As a consequence, the singular form of the noun for deity (*el*) was still used occassionally during and after the monarchy to signify Israel's God, especially in poetic literature which preserved traditional language. But ordinarily (and perplexingly), the Israelites preferred to use the plural form (*elohim*) for deity rather than the singular when speaking of their covenant God.

Perhaps the increasingly henotheistic Israelites began avoiding the singular form of the word for deity (*el*) because of its obvious association with the supreme Canaanite god, El. For whatever reason, they persisted in the unusual practice of using the plural form for deity even after II Isaiah began explicitly teaching them exclusive monotheism c. 540 B.C. at Babylon (See Is. 44:6-8; 45:6-7. II Isaiah was the "second" of a number of prophets who made additions to the book of Isaiah. These later amplifiers considered themselves to be disciples of the prophet Isaiah. Chapters 40-55 are attributed to II Isaiah).

Israel's understanding of the plural form for deity as *exclusively* singular in meaning was probably preceded by an earlier stage which heard it as a broadly henotheistic reference to the "council" of the gods over whom Yahweh reigned as king (Pss. 89:5-7; 95:3; 135:5; 136:2). The day arrived, however, when a devout and concerned henotheist like the Yahwist grew uneasy with an ambiguous plural noun for God which might allow Solomon (and those of like mind) to think that Yahweh's exclusive covenant right to worship in Israel could somehow be shared with other gods.

To make sure that the creation story which introduced the history he was writing for Solomon could not be understood in such a polytheizing way, the Yahwist placed the *personal* name for the God of Israel (Yahweh) in front of the plural form of the word for God (*elohim*) throughout almost all of the story. The only place where he did not do so is the brief dialog between the tempting serpent and the woman (3:1-5). We shall discover later that the Yahwist intended the serpent and the woman as symbols of polytheistic perversion, and on their lips he meant the plural word for God to have a truly polytheistic ring.

Combining the words "Yahweh" and "elohim" as a designation for the God of Israel is unusual; the Yahwist's creation account is the only narrative in the Hebrew scriptures where it occurs. It seems reasonable, therefore, to judge that the Yahwist himself is responsible for it.

7.

AFTER GOD CREATED THE MAN, we are told he planted a garden filled with delightful fruit trees in Eden, "in the east," and there he put the man "to till it and keep it" (2:8-9, 15. Again it is assumed that the first occupation of humans was farming.) The word "Eden" was formerly thought to derive from an Akkadian word meaning "plain," but recent scholarship suggests it probably stems from a West Semitic root and means "place of abundant water." And, indeed, a river of such abundance flowed through the supernaturally fertile garden that as it left the garden it divided into four rivers (2:10), which watered the whole world as imagined by the storyteller.

To fully appreciate what the story is relating about the four rivers (2:11-14), we must remember that the word "Mesopotamia" derives from two Greek words, *mesos* (in the middle, between) and *potamoi* (rivers), and means "land between the rivers," the rivers, of course, being the Tigris to the east and Euphrates to the west. We should also recall that (1) in the early ancient world, everything important finds its *beginning* in the archetypal east (2:8), where the day *begins* at sunrise, and that (2) impressive natural phenomena occurring in *fours* (e.g., the four winds of heaven) are usually meant as encompassing the whole world.

The storyteller proceeds to name and locate some renowned river, which he probably thinks bounds Mesopotamia to the east (2:11, possibly the Indus) and then does the same for the one he thinks bounds the west (2:12, possibly the Nile). He next names and locates, now certainly to the east, the first of two rivers much closer to his own locale, the Tigris (2:14a). Finally, moving westward again, he names, but does not locate the Euphrates (2:14b). We may surmise that he did not bother to locate the Euphrates because he and his community lived in a city or town situated on or near that river; its location was obvious to all.

The information about the four rivers was probably added by either the original mythmaker or some later Mesopotamian expander of the myth. A number of exegetes have observed that the information interrupts the natural flow of the story and requires the repetition in 2:15 of information already given in 2:8. But one occasionally suspects that ancient storytellers were not nearly so averse to repetition, nor keen about economy of statement as some scholars maintain. It is also possible, therefore, that the original mythmaker decided to interrupt his story to inform his community about their relation to Eden and the four rivers, and then resumed the story with a bit of redundancy to get back in context.

The traditional story related that the tree of life (a symbol of the gift of immortality) was in the midst of the garden (2:9b), along with the tree of the knowledge of good and evil (symbolizing a test of the man's willingness to trust and obey God). The man is instructed by God that if he eats the fruit of the second tree (2:17) he will be punished with death (eventual, not immediate), implying he will no longer be allowed to eat the fruit of the tree of life.

At this point in the traditional story, the man was tempted in some way that promised *equality* with God if he ate the forbidden fruit (3:22), and he succumbed. We cannot say with certainty precisely what form his temptation took because the Yahwist extensively revised the temptation story presently found in 3:1-7. It seems likely, however, in view of 3:22-24, that the man was tempted by the serpent in essentially the same way the woman is in the Yahwist's later version (3:1-7).

This conclusion is also supported indirectly by the Gilgamesh epic from ancient Mesopotamia, which relates that the legendary hero, Gilgamesh, was deprived of the power of unending life (obtained from the continued eating of a supernatural plant) through the cunning of a *serpent*. In antiquity, the serpent was often presented as the guardian of the power of immortality, probably because its ability to annually shed its skin led to the popular belief that it could renew its life unendingly and was, therefore, immortal.

8.

WHETHER OR NOT THE YAHWIST found the serpent already present in the traditional account which he revised, he certainly assigned a different meaning to it than the Mesopotamian mythmaker would have. The reasons for this statement are complex and require some background information to be understood.

At the time of the Yahwist, the land of Israel still harbored many Canaanites who had submitted to the authority of David and Solomon. Most of these Canaanites lived in enclaves among the Israelites and continued to practice the polytheistic fertility cult which was an inseparable part of the cult-ivation of their fields. When the Israelites settled in the land, they learned about farming from the Canaanites, who believed that a greater yield from flock and field could be obtained by worshiping gods who specialized in fecundation. Israelite farmers, therefore, were constantly tempted to farm like the Canaanites by worshiping fertility gods. (We should keep in mind that most of the gods worshiped by Solomon's foreign wives also specialized in fertility.)

Ritual practices involving "suggestive" magic were an important part of the worship of fertility gods. The Canaanites believed, for example, that the storm god, Baal, had to renew his sacred marriage with the goddess of fertility (variously called Anith, Astarte, or Asherah) and had to fertilize her in the form of rain to make the earth fruitful. To encourage Baal to do so, the Canaanites resorted to the practice of "ritual" prostitution. They believed that sexual intercourse with a cult prostitute who served at a fertility shrine had magical power to gain Baal's attention and "suggest" that he unite in hierogamy (sacred marriage) with his divine consort so that the blessings of fertility would flow.

A prominent feature of the cult practiced at fertility shrines was ritual *nudity* naively intended, along with ritual copulation, to arouse the fertility gods and "suggest" that they unite in hierogamy. (The goddess of fertility, for related reasons, was always depicted as nude.) Also featured was the ritual handling of *serpents* regarded as phallic symbols of Baal's divine fertilizing power.

With this background in mind, we can appreciate the symbolic associations which the Yahwist intended by his revision of the temptation scene. He went out of his way to associate *nakedness* with the tempting *serpent* (probably present in the original account) to insure that the serpent would now call to mind the worship of fertility gods, which he regarded as Israel's (and Solomon's) most serious temptation. The tree of the knowledge of "good and evil," which promises specious "wisdom" that will make one *equal* with the gods (*elohim*), now additionally symbolizes "knowledge" derived from tasting the forbidden fruit of fertility cult, which purportedly bestows mastery over life and fertility in partnership with the gods of fecundation.

The Yahwist decided to introduce the theme of nakedness in 2:25 ("And the man and his wife were both naked, and were not ashamed"), just after the relocated account of the woman's creation from the man's rib in 2:22-24. The story's chapter divisions make it seem that 2:25 is the *conclusion* of chapter two, but the chapter divisions were not added until the thirteenth century A.D., and are sometimes misleading. In reality, we can tell from the wordplay in the Hebrew text between the word "naked" (*arummim*), used *enclosingly* in 2:25 and 3:7, and the word "cunning" (*arum*) in 3:1, that 2:25 was intended by the Yahwist as his *introduction* to the temptation scene which follows immediately in 3:1-7.

As soon as the man consents to his wife's enticement and eats the forbidden fruit (3:6), the Yahwist returns to the theme of nakedness introduced in 2:25, and announces that now "their eyes were opened, and they knew that they were naked" (*arummim* 3:7). He deliberately connected *nakedness* with the sin and shame instigated by the cunning (*arum*) *serpent* to suggest that participation in foreign fertility cult, with its ritual nudity and serpent-handling, is a shameful violation of Israel's covenant with her God.

9.

AFTER THE MAN AND HIS WIFE fall into sin, the Yahwist relates that God comes looking for the guilty pair, and they try to hide among the trees. When God inquires about their conduct, the man acknowledges that they hid because they were "naked" (3:10). God then observes (3:11) that if "knowledge" of their nakedness includes guilt and shame, they must have eaten the forbidden fruit (now a symbol of unlawful "knowledge" obtained from participation in fertility cult).

In recognizably human fashion, the man blames the woman, who, in turn, blames the serpent (3:12-13). A solemn cursing of the three culprits then follows in the order of their contribution to the crime. Whereas the narrative of the temptation and fall had to be carefully reworked by the editorializing Yahwist, the solemn poetry of the three curses (3:14-19) is entirely the product of his own faith inspired purpose.

The serpent is first to be cursed (3:14-15), and the words of its condemnation are deployed to teach Solomon (and Israel) an urgent religious lesson. The God of Israel declares that he intends to wage war against the serpent (fertility cult) and its seed (those who serve fertility gods) through the primordial woman (Eve) and her "seed" (an elect people destined to descend from her). For through the woman's childbearing power, God will eventually bring *Israel* into being as the people chosen to be his instrument in crushing the detestable fertility cult (3:15b) in which foreign gods compete with him, the true source of fertility and blessing, for humankind's devotion (Gen. 12:1-3).

There is, as indicated above, an admonition for King Solomon in all of this. As God's anointed representative on earth, he is especially responsible for upholding the covenant between Israel and her God. It is Solomon above all others in Israel who is the woman's "seed" destined to attack and eliminate unlawful fertility cult instead of officially condoning it in the case of his foreign wives (See 2 Sam. 7:12 where Solomon is alluded to as the woman's "seed" as well as David's.) The Yahwist and his collaborators hoped that none of this religious "wisdom" would be lost on Solomon, renowned for his worldly "wisdom" (1 Kgs. 3:9-28).

The woman is next to be cursed (3:16): She is told that in addition to death she must endure the pain of childbirth as punishment for her role in her husband's sin. When God concludes by "patriarchally" admonishing the woman that her husband shall "rule over" her, it is probable that the Yahwist is guardedly suggesting that King Solomon should properly exercise his royal and husbandly authority by ruling over (or overruling) his foreign wives in matters of religion.

Finally, the man is cursed (3:17-19) with wrathful words intended also, and even primarily, as a warning for Solomon:

> Because you have listened to the voice of your wife,
> and have eaten of the tree of which I commanded

you, 'You shall not eat of it,' cursed is the ground
because of you. . . . (3:17)

The man is also told that he must now toil arduously for
his bread until death returns him to the dust from which
he was formed.

In verse 3:20 the man gives the name Eve to his wife.
The Hebrew word translated as "Eve" is of uncertain
meaning, but on the basis of context and popular etymo-
logy the story implies that the name expresses admiration
for the woman's ability to give life through childbearing.
Because the woman's name is archaic and of uncertain
meaning, it was probably found by the Yahwist in the traditional account of the woman's creation which he relocated.

With the appearance of the famous Greek translation of
the Hebrew scriptures called the Septuagint (c. 250 B.C.),
it became customary to begin transliterating the Hebrew
word for "human being" (*adam*) into the personal name
"Adam" somewhere in the second chapter of Genesis. The
Septuagint translator(s) began in 2:16; St. Jerome, in his
influential Latin Vulgate translation (c. 405 A.D.), chose
to begin in 2:19; his decision was followed by the Douay
and King James versions, both completed by 1610 A.D.
The currently popular Revised Standard Version introduces the name "Adam" in 3:19.

It is probable that all of these versions share, consciously or unconsciously, the patriarchal conviction that
the man should be given a personal name *before* he names
the animals in 2:19 and his wife in 3:20. However, in the
more ancient Hebrew text (and its still more ancient Mesopotamian predecessor), culturally conditioned bias
worked the opposite way; some of the archaic awe once
generated in matriarchal societies by the belief that
women conceived their offspring solely by female magic
(unassisted by men) lingers on in the honorific bestowed
on the woman by her husband, who remains nameless.

Several recent versions have avoided using the name "Adam" in the creation stories to more accurately reflect the Hebrew text.

Since it was the Yahwist who introduced the theme of shameful or guilt-causing nakedness earlier in the narrative, it is probably he who tells us in 3:21 that God made garments of skin for the man and his wife and clothed them. The Mesopotamian mythmaker is unlikely to have experienced a need to cover their nakedness since ritual nudity was an acceptable part of his cultural tradition. (But not so in Israel; see Exod. 20:26.) God's providential clothing of the guilty pair further conveys the Yahwist's conviction that God, in his mercy, has forgiven humankind and has a limited (temporal) plan of salvation for them to be accomplished through the woman and her "seed" (3:15).

In a final, ironic declaration (3:22), God states, with feigned surprise, that "the man has become like one of us, knowing good and evil." These words imply that instead of attaining true "wisdom" and equality with God as promised by the serpent, the man's folly has condemned him to suffering and death. The unusual plural pronoun in God's declaration is a vestige of the originally polytheistic account; it was probably spared excision because of traditional delight in the declaration's sarcasm. Such plural language was tolerated by the Yahwist as either a plural of majesty (Yahweh speaks in the plural like the great kings of the earth), or a divine address to a council of angelic ministers (1 Kgs. 22:19-23). For the reasons given above, the Yahwist would no longer have allowed the older henotheistic view that such plural language implied Yahweh addressing the "council of the gods" with supreme authority.

God then obliquely reminds the man (with sustained irony) that, as forewarned, he may no longer eat the fruit of the tree of life and enjoy freedom from death (3:22). The man is forthwith driven from the garden, and a fearsome pair of minor deities called cherubim is posted at the garden's entrance "to guard the way to the tree of life" (3:23). We are told in addition that a "flaming sword" (probably a supernatural sword with a lightning bolt for a blade) was also placed at the garden's entrance (3:24) to assist the cherubim: any who might violate the sacred precinct by attempting to steal the fruit of the tree of life would be incinerated.

The Yahwist allowed the traditional myth's melancholy conclusion to stand unchanged. He evidently agreed with the Mesopotamian mythmaker's judgment that, because of some primordial failure, humans are forever bereft of hope for everlasting life. He believed that if Israel and the House of David cooperated with God's plan of salvation, a Golden Age in the form of unprecedented peace, prosperity, and length of life, could come for all nations. But, as the Yahwist understood it, God's plan of salvation did not include the restoration of everlasting life.

Questions for Further Study

1. What special set of historical circumstances motivated the Yahwist to write his account of the creation and fall?

2. What internal evidence in the Yahwist's account indicates that originally only the first man was tempted in the garden and disobeyed God?

3. What important function does a myth have in the lives of ancient human communities?

4. What important distinction about invisible causal power have ancient mythmakers not yet learned to make?

5. What fundamentally correct insight is always being expressed by a myth?

6. What serious problem in his historical experience was the Mesopotamian mythmaker trying to explain by

teaching that the first human was tested by God and failed the test?

7. What is unusual about the Hebrew noun for God that was customarily used by the ancient Israelites?

8. What is it about the way the four rivers are named in the Yahwist's account which indicates that the original form of the story was created by a mythmaker who lived in Mesopotamia?

9. What symbolic meaning did the Mesopotamian mythmaker attach to the two special trees in the middle of the garden?

10. What symbolic meaning did the Yahwist attach to the serpent and the guilt-causing nakedness of the humans in his revised temptation scene?

11. What symbolic meaning did the Yahwist attach to the serpent's "seed" when he narrated the cursing of the serpent in 3:15?

12. What symbolic meaning did the Yahwist attach to the Woman's "seed" when he narrated the cursing of the serpent in 3:15?

Part Three: The Priestly Author's Account

1.

WE WILL NOW TURN OUR THOUGHTS to the second of the two creation stories, the one written by the Priestly Author c. 500 B.C. at Babylon. King Nebuchadnezzer of Babylonia subdued the rebellious kingdom of Judah and destroyed Jerusalem in 587 B.C.; he then took the remaining members of the ruling class and most of the surviving inhabitants of Jerusalem as captives to the city of Babylon.

In the bitter pain of their exile, the Judaites remembered Jeremiah the prophet's promise that God would forgive them and bring them back to their homeland in seventy years (Jer. 29:10-15). In order to win God's approval and secure that promise, they began to study the Law of Moses and the writings of the Prophets with new commitment, especially on their traditional Sabbath day.

In fact, Cyrus the Persian conquered Babylonia and took Babylon without resistance in 539 B.C.; the following year he gave the deportees from *Judah* (now increasingly referred to as *Jews*) permission to return to their homeland forty-nine years after their exile had begun. However, since permission to rebuild the walls of war-ravaged Jerusalem was denied, most of the Jews chose to settle within the massive walls of Babylon, where they had physical and economic security. This situation presented the Priestly Author with a special challenge. By that time, he and the Jews in Babylon had been taught by II Isaiah to understand and practice exclusive monotheism (Is. 44:6-8; 45:5-7). The Priestly Author was clearly aware of the superiority of recently introduced Jewish monotheism (Is. 44: 9-20), but was nevertheless worried about the seductive power of Babylon's glittering polytheistic culture.

Babylon was considered the most beautiful city in the Ancient Near East; its imposing walls contained the celebrated hanging gardens, magnificent temples, and splendid palaces. The material achievement of Babylon was undeniably impressive, and the Priestly author feared that the Jews might be tempted to abandon their newly found monotheistic faith, with its stern ethical demands, in favor of the material prosperity ostensibly bestowed by the gods of Babylon.

Babylon's power to dazzle would have become especially intense every springtime when the new year festival was celebrated with twelve days of spectacular pageantry. During this celebration, the polytheistic Babylonian myth which recounted the creation of the world by the victorious god Marduk was solemnly recited and perhaps dramatically reenacted.

This solemn recital of the creation myth was an essential part of the ritual deemed necessary to guarantee the renewal of creation and its annual cycle for the coming year. The Jews living in Babylon can hardly have failed to learn about the twelve day festival and its creation myth, and curiosity in the young being what it is, some probably joined the festivities as spectators, others, possibly, as worshipers.

In his pastoral zeal to insure that Jews would preserve their monotheistic faith amid the temptations of Babylon, the Priestly Author devised a plan to encourage them to faithfully gather on the Sabbath for prayer and readings from the law and the prophets: He decided to write a new creation account as a preface to the old Yahwistic story. The Priestly Author's purpose in writing this new account was twofold: (1) he wished to encourage Sabbath observance as a means of preserving monotheistic Jewish faith, and (2) he wanted to present the Jewish community with an impressive monotheistic creation account that would effectively counteract the Babylonian account by depriving it of credibility.

2.

TO ENCOURAGE SABBATH OBSERVANCE, the Priestly Author decided to present God's creative activity within a *seven-day* framework. He described God as engaged in the specific works of creation for six consecutive days and then declared solemnly (and redundantly) that on the *seventh* day God rested from all his labors, thereby providing a divine precedent for the observance of the seventh day (the Sabbath) as a hallowed time of rest set apart for worship of the one true God (Gen 2:2-3).

The Priestly Author's attainment of his second goal, the repudiation and replacement of the Babylonian creation account, was a bit more complicated. We will better understand why he proceeded with his task as he did if we are familiar with the general outline of the Babylonian creation story, the Enuma elish. In that account, the victorious god Marduk created the world from the colossal carcass of Tiamat, the great goddess identified with the primordial sea; it was she and her husband, Apsu (identified with the primordial river flowing phallically into the sea), who were the ultimate progenitors of all the gods.

When Tiamat threatened to destroy a large number of her divine offspring, Marduk successfully engaged her in battle, inflicted a mortal wound, and divided her corpse into halves. With one half he created the vault of heaven (the firmament), and with the other, the earth. Marduk then appointed stations in heaven for the gods and permanent places for the starry constellations that represented them. He also established the months, seasons, and years by creating fixed pathways for the Sun god who ruled the day and the Moon goddess who ruled the night. Finally, after consulting the god Ea, renowned for wisdom, Marduk created humans from the blood of Kingu (a god who had been allied with Tiamat, and was also defeated and slain by Marduk).

Marduk created humans so that the gods might be free from the burden of providing their own sustenance; humans, therefore, were assigned the task of growing food for the gods and providing daily meals for them on the altars of their temples on earth.

3.

THE PRIESTLY AUTHOR'S MONOTHEISTIC ACCOUNT of creation frequently reacts in subtle ways to things stated in the Babylonian account, always intending to negate the account's polytheism. He begins by telling us that before God began to create, the earth was shrouded in darkness and covered by a primordial sea (1:1-2), which reminds us of the role of Tiamat's watery carcass in the Babylonian story. As we would expect, Tiamat is not mentioned by the Priestly author, but his word for the "deep sea" (*tehom*) that covers the earth (1:2a) reminds us indirectly (and unintendedly) of her role in the Babylonian myth.

We are told that the "Spirit of God" (not the creative power of Marduk) was moving in readiness over the waters (1:2b), awaiting God's creative command. The

Hebrew word for "Spirit" (*ruach*) basically means "wind" or "breath," but can also mean "Spirit," depending on its context. And while it is true that the worldview of the Priestly Author was such that he could use one word to signify all three of these invisible realities, it is also true that we cannot. We may justifiably infer that when the Priestly Author uses the word "ruach" in his story in connection with God's creative activity, he intends it to be understood as the invisible creative power (Spirit) of God about to be directed by the Divine command which will recur during the following six days.

On the *first* day God calls forth light from the encompassing darkness and names the light, day, and the darkness, night (1:3-5a). Ancient Israel reckoned that a day ended with sunset, and that in the ensuing night the next day was already present, ready to emerge in full view at sunrise. For this reason, the Jewish tradition begins its Sabbath (Saturday) observance on Friday evening after sunset, and considers the Sabbath to be completed when the sun sets on Saturday evening. Accordingly, a solemn formula is used by the Priestly Author to call attention to the end of each of the six days of creation leading up to the divinely inaugurated *seventh* day of rest: "And there was evening and there was morning, one day" (1:5, see 1:8, 13, 19, 23, 31).

On the *second* day God creates the solid vault of heaven called the "firmament" (1:7). Its purpose is to separate and hold back the waters above heaven (which periodically fall through opened floodgates in the form of rain) from the waters still covering the earth below (1:7). The Babylonian account also mentions the vault of heaven, but says that Marduk created it from one of the halves of Tiamat's corpse.

On the *third* day God causes the dry land to emerge from the waters below the firmament (1:9-10), and creates the various kinds of vegetation on earth that produce fruit containing seed (1:11-12). It is clear that the Priestly Author and his community are still close enough to the discovery of agriculture to be fascinated by the mysterious nature of seeds. A sense of wonder resonates in his repeated reference to God's creation of "fruit trees bearing fruit in which is their seed, each according to its kind" (1:11-12).

The Babylonian creation story makes no mention of the creation of plants and trees by Marduk; their presence is merely implied when humans are assigned the task of providing food for the gods. By explicitly ascribing the creation of all green growing things to the one true God, the Priestly Author is reminding the ancient Jews that the one true God is the only source of the vegetation that all higher forms of life on earth depend on; vegetation is not provided annually by fertility gods.

On the *fourth* day God creates the great lights that travel across the firmament, separating day from night and determining the months, seasons, and years (1:14-15). We are then redundantly and emphatically told that it is *God* who made the two great lights, "the greater light to rule the day and the lesser light to rule the night; he made the stars also" (1:16). The Priestly author stresses that the sun, moon, and stars were *created* by the only true God because the Babylonian myth related that when Marduk established the seasons and the times he merely created fixed paths to be followed by the Sun god, the Moon goddess, and the Wandering Stars (i.e., planets, believed to be divine beings who wandered the starry heavens) all of whom existed *before* creation.

The Priestly Author deliberately avoids using the Hebrew words for "sun" and "moon" to further specify "the two great lights" because these words were also personal names for the astral deities who "ruled" over the day and night throughout the Ancient Near East. It is noteworthy that even though he is trying to avoid polytheistic lan-

guage by speaking of "the two great lights," the Priestly
Author's fund of monotheistic language is still so new and
limited that he describes the great lights as ruling over
day and night, echoing polytheistic belief that astral di-
vinities *rule* over historical destiny.

Even though light was created and separated from darkness on the first day (1:4), the creation of "the two great
lights" which also separate light from darkness (1:18) was
probably deferred till the fourth day because of the importance of astral deities and astrology among the Babylonians
(Is. 47:1,13). The Priestly Author avoided connecting the
sun, moon, and wandering stars with the beginning of creation on the first day as a further way of rejecting
Babylonian belief that they already existed as divine beings before the world began.

On the *fifth* day God creates "the swarms of living
creatures" that swim in the seas below (1:22), those that
fly through the sky above (1:22), and those that creep
and move upon the earth (1:25). He then blesses the living creatures by commanding them to "be fruitful and
multiply," which again reminds the ancient Jews that
the one true God is the *sole* source of life and blessing,
not the gods of fertility mistakenly worshiped by other
nations.

On the *sixth* day God reaches the pinnacle of his creative purpose and creates human beings. At this point in
the Priestly Author's account, something astonishing occurs. Whereas in the Yahwist's account God mocks the
disobedient humans because they had foolishly presumed
to become "like" God ("Behold, the man has become like
one of us. . . ." 3:22), the Priestly Author introduces a
dramatic *reversal* of this earlier divine scorn by having
God himself now declare (using the same surprising plural pronouns found in 3:22): "Let us make man in our
image, after our likeness" (1:26). What prompted this divine change of attitude?

The Priestly Author probably wished to remind the Jews that the one true God had called them through the law of Moses to a life of *holiness* in his service ("You must be holy, for I the Lord your God am holy," Lev. 19:2. See also 20:26; 21:6, 8). In addition, just before King Cyrus delivered them from captivity in 538 B.C., God had again called them through the prophet II Isaiah to be his servant-people (41:8-10; 44:21) and witness (43:10) to his *oneness* (44:6-8) and *holiness* (43:15; 47:4) among the nations.

To encourage the Jews to undertake their lofty vocation of witnessing to the one true God and "imaging" his holiness among the nations by the uprightness and holiness of their lives, the Priestly Author decided that he must *counteract* the earlier view that it is absurd for frail humans made of clay to aspire to be "like" God. Instead of stressing the physical frailty of humans, the Priestly Author chose to emphasize our privileged possession of the creative power of reason and freedom of choice which enables us to cooperate with God's creative purpose and share responsibly in his "dominion" over the kingdom of creation. (Notice that since the demise of the monarchy, it is no longer primarily the king, but God's covenant people, who are called to share in God's oversight of the kingdom of creation).

Accordingly, the Priestly Author presents a majestic account of God announcing his intention to make humans in his own "image" and "likeness" (1:26) so they may share in his divine "dominion" over creation (1:28). To call attention to his inspired reversal of the earlier view in 3:22, the Priestly Author deliberately imitates its primitive *plural* pronouns even as he alters its negative meaning with sublime new intent.

Placing *plural* pronouns in the mouth of God in an otherwise rigorously monotheistic account was countenanced by the Priestly Author only because of the urgency of his theological task and his realization that such plural language could be understood as the plural of majesty. The plural of majesty is probably the only interpretation of the plural pronouns he would have allowed since the advent of monotheism meant the eclipse of henotheism, and angels are *never* mentioned in the Pentateuchal material attributed to the Priestly author and his editorial cohorts. Even so, we can tell that the Priestly Author was still uneasy about using the *plural* language necessary to make his point in 1:26 ("Let us make man in our image, after our likeness"), for in 1:27, *lest anyone misunderstand,* he immediately repeats the same thought, but now carefully replaces the plural with *singular* pronouns ("So God created man in his own image, in the image of God he created him; male and female he created them").

After creating the humans, God bestows his special blessing by commanding them to "be fruitful and multiply, and fill the earth and subdue it"; he then confers upon them "dominion over the fish of the sea and over the birds of the air and over every living thing that moves upon the earth" (1:28). Finally, God gives the humans permission to eat plants and fruits for nourishment (1:29); the animals are also allowed green plants for food (1:30). The Priestly Author taught that before the arrival and spread of sin there was no violence or bloodshed on earth; it is his view that humans and animals were vegetarians and herbivores before the fall.

In the Priestly Author's religious interpretation of history, humans were not given permission to kill animals and eat their flesh until after the great flood when God made a covenant with Noah (Gen. 9:3). In the Yahwist's account of God's rebuke of the man, there is also a brief directive restricting the human diet to plants (3:18). But since nothing like the concern of this directive occurs elsewhere in the Yahwist's writings, and it disrupts the otherwise related thoughts that precede and follow it, we may reasonably suspect its editorial insertion by the Priestly Author, who was obviously concerned about this matter (1:29-30; 9:3-4) and the observance of dietary laws in general. He probably added the dietary directive to 3:18 in the Yahwist's account when he prefaced it with his new creation story. He wished to imply by this strategy that dietary laws had been part of God's purpose for humankind from the very beginning.

During the course of each of the first five days, except the second, God finds that what he has made is "good" (1:4, 10, 12, 18, 21, 25). But on the sixth day, when God has completed his creative labors, he surveys the results of the past six days and finds all he has wrought to be "very good" (1:31). The Priestly Author is thereby affirming the fundamental goodness of the gift of creation (1:31), and probably also rejecting the polytheistic violence that permeates creation in the Babylonian account (Tiamat's sundered corpse, Kingu's blood).

When the climactic *seventh* day arrives, we are told with great solemnity that God "rested from all his labors," and that he "hallowed" or sanctified the seventh day, setting it apart for his own worship as Creator. The Priestly Author, having achieved his purpose of demonstrating the monotheistc origin of the world and the divine institution of the Sabbath, tersely notifies us that his account is finished: "These are the generations of the heavens and the earth when they were created" (2:4a).

It has possibly occurred to the reflective reader that it was odd for the Priestly Author to have allowed his account to spill over into the beginning of chapter 2, where it ends awkwardly at verse 4a. Mention has already been made that originally there were no chapter divisions in the Bible. The chapter divisions presently found there are thought to have been added by an English bishop named Stephen Langton (who signed Magna Carta) in the thirteenth century of the Christian era. The verse numbers now in use were not supplied until the sixteenth century. This information enables us to understand the unseemly divisions we occasionally find in the Bible. Those responsible had the best of intentions, but sometimes lacked a sufficiently informed understanding of the text.

We have now concluded our examination of the historical influences and religious concerns that contributed to the formation of the Genesis creation accounts. In the remaining sections we will turn our attention to their significance for our present faith understanding.

Questions for Further Study

1. Why did the Priestly author consider ancient Babylon a source of special temptation for the ancient Jews residing there after the Exile?

2. For what two important reasons did the Priestly Author write a new creation story as a preface to the old one?

3. Why did the Priestly Author describe the creative activity of God within a seven-day framework?

4. Why did the Priestly author say that God created the "two great lights" instead of being more clear and saying that he created the "sun and the moon"?

5. If the Priestly Author was striving to write a strictly monotheistic creation story, why did he use plural pronouns in 1:26 where God declares his intention to make humans "in our image, after our likeness"?

Part Four: Abiding Relevance

1.

WHEN NONSPECIALISTS BECOME ACQUAINTED with the modern reading of the Genesis creation stories, they frequently judge that since the accounts were written to address unusual faith problems in the distant past, they are no longer relevant for our faith needs today. Such a response is understandable but mistaken. There are a number of good reasons why the creation stories will continue to express vital meaning for all later ages.

To begin with, the stories provide an illuminating record of the dedicated and creative ways that our spiritual forebears struggled to remain faithful to the advanced understanding of God that they had attained. For example, it is instructive to observe the Priestly Author groping for the new language needed to teach and defend the monotheistic faith he and his community had only recently arrived at. His was an extremely important task at a critical moment in the history of religion, and we are the spiritual beneficiaries of his achievement.

Likewise, one is filled with admiration for the ingenuity and commitment manifested by the Yahwist in his earlier, but no less important mission of defending Israel's superior henotheistic faith from the regressive tug of polytheism and the scandalous behavior of King Solomon. It is evident that the Yahwist and the Priestly Author were inspired by their advanced understanding of God to write on his behalf. Their inspired words are part of the sacred history through which God has manifested himself to us in a special way to prepare us for his definitive Self-communication in the Christ Event. Without the faith commitment manifested by the Yahwist and the Priestly Author, we might not be Christian monotheists today. To the degree that we fail to understand and appreciate their inspired contributions to God's unfolding Self-disclosure in history, our own understanding of God is impoverished.

Our appreciation should also reach back a step further and include the contribution of the Mesopotamian mythmaker who taught the earliest form of the traditional story revised by the Yahwist. We should recognize that he also was "inspired" by his faith experience of Ultimate Causality (interpreted polytheistically) to provide his contemporaries with an account of Creation and its tragic disruption by sin.

His story was an important earlier step in the process by which humankind has striven to articulate an understanding of the genesis of all things, including evil. It is striking to realize that in the first three chapters of Genesis we find evidence of the polytheistic, henotheistic, and monotheistic stages through which human thinking about the mystery of God has evolved.

2.

IN ADDITION TO THEIR HISTORICAL VALUE, the creation stories contain a timeless religious message even after we have learned they were not divinely dictated and should not be taken literally. All we need do is shift mental gears and learn to read the stories symbolically. We will then discover that they still contain a number of wise insights essential for becoming authentically human.

The suggestion that some portions of the Bible should be understood nonliterally or symbolically still meets with considerable misunderstanding. This problem arises from the popular misconception that what is "literally" true is *really* true, and what is "symbolically" true is *not* really true. This mistaken attitude is symptomatic of the empirical bias that typifies our age.

Poets, philosophers, and theologians have long known that we can only make "literal" statements about *empirical* experience (that derived through our five senses), and that we humans have our most important experiences (reason, freedom, justice, love, commitment, human dignity, and, most importantly, God) on the *transempirical* level (that which lies beyond the empirical surface of things and is implicit in their depths).

Transempirical realities are not empirically demonstrable, but they are *experientially* verifiable. We cannot demonstrate the existence of freedom of choice, yet we all *experience* the agony of making the right decision in certain critical situations. In the judgment of most humans, the most important realities in our total range of experience are transempirical in nature. But since we cannot directly perceive or observe them, we cannot make "literal" statements about them. Because of their crucial importance in our lives, however, we must speak about them. When we do, we employ "symbolic" comparisons which enable us to illustrate inferred realities with the aid of things directly and clearly perceived.

Since God's reality is known through intuition and inference, not by empirical observation, it follows that everything we say about God and the God-human relationship is necessarily symbolic or figurative. But this should not surprise or trouble us, for Jesus himself indicates that we must proceed in the symbolic mode when speaking of transcendent realities: "To what may we compare the kingdom of God, or what parable may we use to illustrate it?" (Mark 4:30; see also Luke 13:20.)

The perceptive reader who recognizes the necessity of expressing higher reality and meaning with symbols will find that the following important truths verified by our *experience* are still present in the "deliteralized" Genesis creation stories:

1. *Our universe did not happen by chance; it was called into being by a Creator, who is the ultimate Source of its order, meaning, and beauty.*

This truth is symbolized by God's creative activity in both creation stories (1:3, 7, 9, 11, 16, 21, 25, 27; 2:7-9, 19, 21-22).

2. *All of creation is fundamentally good and points to the goodness of its ultimate Source.*

This truth is expressed in the Priestly Author's account when God observes throughout the six days of creation that what he has made is good (1:4, 12, 18, 25), and finally, very good (1:31).

3. *We humans bring moral evil and tragic suffering into the world by misusing our freedom in ways contrary to our Creator's purpose.*

This truth is indicated in the Yahwist's account when the humans experience guilt and self-alienation after disobeying God, and try to hide themselves among the trees (3:7-11).

4. *Our life has been given to us as a gift; but a genuine gift is always a sign of love, which implies that our Creator created us out of love, and enduringly loves us.*

God's abiding love for us is implied when he makes garments for the man and his wife and clothes them, even after they have sinned (3:21).

5. *Since we humans possess the special gifts of reason and freedom of choice, we are responsible for distinguishing good from evil and choosing what is truly good.*

This truth is implied when the humans are tested by God's command not to eat from the tree of the knowledge of "good and evil" (2:17), and also when they are rebuked by God for having done so (3:16-17).

6. *It is our possession of the* creative power *of reason and freedom of choice that makes us the "image" of our* Creator.

This truth is indicated when God, after creating humans in his image and likeness (1:26), assigns them "dominion," or power to govern responsibly as God's earthly representatives, over the kingdom of creation (1:28).

7. *Because we are the image of God, we humans are the most important creatures in the universe. In a very real sense, everything else prepares for us and was created for our sake.*

The *first* truth is implied when God creates only the humans in his image and likeness and gives them sole dominion over creation (1:26-28); it is also implied by the man's superior power to name the other creatures in the garden (2:19).

The *second* truth is suggested when God creates the humans on the sixth day as the culmination of his creative purpose, and, since they alone are his "image," gives them dominion over all that led up to them (2:26-28).

8. *Because we humans share creative power with our* Creator, *we are responsible for "imaging" (i.e., exemplifying and making credible) his creative love in the world.*

This truth is rather subtle, but is implied in the Priestly Author's account when he reverses the pejorative view of humans expressed in the Yahwist's earlier account in order to encourage the ancient Jews to witness responsibly to God's oneness and holiness among the nations (1:26-28).

9. *Our possession of the creative power of reason and freedom of choice implies that we are especially responsible for cooperating with the purpose of our Creator by completing that part of creation left unfinished and entrusted to us, i.e., ourselves.*

This truth is suggested by the test of obedience required by God of the humans in the garden (2:16-17). The story implies that God holds them responsible for cooperating with his creative purpose if they are to permanently enjoy the power of everlasting life.

10. *We are authentically human only when we act in ways that create and enhance life in cooperation with our Creator rather than destroy or diminish it.*

This truth, again, is subtle, but implied by the positive condition of the humans while they are still living in responsible harmony with God's creative design, as opposed to their diminished condition (i.e., guilty, self-alienated, and other-alienated) after their willful violation of God's purpose (2:25 vs. 3:7-13).

11. *We self-transcending humans have been destined for everlasting life and friendship with God from the very beginning of our existence.*

This truth is symbolized by the intimate relationship that the humans enjoyed with God in the garden before the fall (3:8), and by their original access to the tree of life (2:16-17).

12. *It is imperative that we humans regularly set time apart for: (a) communicating with our Creator, (b) thinking about the creative task he has*

assigned us, and (c) recognizing how we might improve the quality of our response to his abiding love.

This truth is clearly indicated by God's solemn consecration of the Sabbath day at the culmination of the Priestly Author's creation account (2:1-3), and God's implied intention that we should "image" his creative love in the world while fulfilling the task of our own self-completion (1:26-28).

13. We humans have always experienced shame and guilt when we violate our conscience and misuse our freedom for selfish and destructive ends.

This truth is implied by the behavior of the man and his wife, who experienced guilt and hid themselves from the presence of God *after* they had eaten the forbidden fruit (3:6-11).

14. We humans are universally troubled by the ambiguous nature of death, and prone to fear that it might be the occasion of everlasting punishment for our past personal failures.

This truth is indicated when we remember that the purpose of the traditional myth used and revised by the Yahwist was to explain the tragic and disturbing necessity of death as the consequence of human moral failure (2:17; 3:19, 24).

15. Our responsible exercise of freedom always involves a struggle with the temptation to inauthenticity.

This truth is suggested by the temptation and fall in the Yahwist's account (3:1-13).

16. We are habitually prone to the regressive worship of "false gods" which lead us away from the self-transcending destiny assigned us by our Creator.

This truth is implied when we remember that the
fundamental purpose motivating both the Yahwist and
the Priestly Author was to prevent Israel from regres-
sively "falling" into the worship of "unworthy" (the Yahwist) or "false" (the Priestly Author) gods. The forbidden
fruit in the Yahwist's account is a symbol of the "false"
worship of unworthy gods which, even for monotheists,
still abound and tempt—money, material possessions,
power, personal acclaim, sex, alcohol, drugs, television,
and any other created thing we can abuse or become irra-
tionally and destructively addicted to.

**17. *Our use of the gift of creation should always be
in responsible harmony with God's creative purpose and goodness.***

This ecological imperative is implicit in the Priestly
Author's teaching that originally, before humans were
wounded by sin, there was no violent shedding of blood on
earth. He assumed that humans and animals alike ate no
meat, but were vegetarians (1:29-30). Only later, and
with special restrictions that reminded them of the sa-
credness of the gift of life, did he think humans were allowed to depart from the standards of original innocence
and kill animals for food (Gen 9:3-6).

The Priestly Author's assumptions about an original state
of innocence in nature are naive and unfounded, yet his conviction that the gift of life is sacred and to be treated with
reverence is certainly true. He reminds us that our Creator
would have us make use of his creation with gratitude and
concern for all other existing things that are part of the
total gift of life. Unnecessary suffering or destruction
should never be inflicted on other created things, all of
which, in varying degrees, participate in the mystery of life
and make our own life possible. Even if eating meat is mor-
ally permissible, there is still a moral and humane way to
raise and butcher animals, as opposed to an immoral and
dehumanizing way. The Priestly Author reminds us that

both our *Creator* and a *creatively* formed conscience (one that truly "images" its Creator) can approve and employ only humane and moral ways of acting.

Questions for Further Study

1. What value is there in studying ancient creation accounts written by authors whose world view was so different from our own?

2. If modern scholarship agrees that the Genesis creation and fall stories should not be taken *literally,* why do we continue to value and read them?

3. For what important reason should Christians not be surprised to learn that spiritual realities can only be spoken of figuratively or symbolically?

4. Which part of creation do the Genesis creation accounts imply that we are especially responsible for completing, and, if we do not do so, no one else can or will?

5. Now that we understand clearly that there is only one God, what value is there for us in the study of creation and fall stories that were primarily intended to discourage the worship of false gods?

Part Five: Remaining Questions

1.

STUDENTS WHO HAVE BEEN TAUGHT the traditional reading of the Genesis creation stories and then become acquainted with the modern reading usually raise a number of predictable questions. Although the answers to most of these questions are implicit in a perceptive reading of the material already presented, those questions most frequently asked will be listed and answered below:

1. **Were Adam and Eve truly the first parents of the human race?**

   The answer to this question (and those following) must necessarily be complex and dialectic, i.e., the answer cannot, by its very nature, be a simple "yes" or "no," but must combine both "yes" and "no" into a new and higher synthesis. Symbolically speaking, the answer is "yes"; literally speaking, it is "no."

   We learned earlier that the names "Adam" and "Eve" are not really the personal names of the first two humans. "Eve" is the symbolic name given to the first woman in the *myth* received and revised by the Yahwist; the name was never biographical in nature. Nor was "Adam" originally a personal name; it is actually the Hebrew word meaning "human being," which was later treated as a name by translators. "Adam" and "Eve," in reality, are personal symbols for the progenitors of the human race. (Remember, behind every symbol stands an experienced reality.)

We know from the scientific study of fossil evidence that the human race did not always exist on earth. It seems to have begun somewhere between two and three million years ago, and most scientists think that its beginning was polygenistic (involving many pairs of first parents) rather than monogenistic (involving only one pair of first parents). If the more likely polygenistic interpretation is correct, then we had "many" first parents who belonged to the branch of hominids that evolved into the first humans.

One way or another, the human race certainly required "first parents." "Adam" and "Eve" are the symbolic names given by the Jewish and Christian traditions to those progenitors.

2. Did the "first parents" of the human race originally possess immortality and special innocence which they later lost?

Historically, there was never a time when humans enjoyed freedom from the biological necessity of death. But there was a time, *psychologically* speaking, when we were all free from the knowledge that we had to die, and we unconsciously presumed (abetted by the mathematically infinite capacity of our self-transcending consciousness) that we would go on experiencing life on earth unendingly. This was the time of dreaming innocence in early childhood. When children eventually discover that they and all others must die, they react with metaphysical shock, and the memory of the occasion is usually repressed unless they are also given a set of positive sym-

bols which assures them that humans can transcend
death.

This background information enables us to understand
the unconscious psychological origin of the mythical symbols in the Yahwist's creation story, and why the story
naively supposes humans were not originally bound by
death. Essentially the same explanation accounts for the
assigning of original innocence to humans before their
fall. Such an attribution is really the unconscious retro-
jection of early childhood innocence into an ideally imagined beginning. The dreaming innocence of early childhood has not yet encountered the moral complexity and
guilt that characterize adulthood; when such complexity
and guilt are eventually experienced, they contribute to
the universal "fall."

3. Did the first parents of the human race actually dwell in the garden of Paradise?

To begin with, the word "Paradise" is not found in the
Hebrew text of Genesis; instead, it speaks of the garden
of "Eden." The word "Paradise" entered the biblical tradition by way of the Greek Septuagint translation (c.
250 B.C.), which used the word *paradeisos* (enclosed
park) to render the Hebrew word for garden.

The garden of Eden or Paradise is a mythological symbol;
it represents the ideal environment where our first parents
were imagined to have lived in a state of immortality and
special innocence before the fall. Neither historically nor
geographically did such a place ever exist; and yet, in another way (psychologically), the human race truly does find
its origin in an *experienced* realm symbolized by that place.
(Again, behind every symbol stands an experienced reality.)

Experientially speaking, the "garden of Paradise" is
the idealized environment of earliest childhood where
normally we are provided for, protected, and loved by
our parents, those "godlike" giants who seem (to help-

less and ignorant infants) to be omniscient and omnipotent. While dwelling in this ideal environment, we ordinarily know nothing of adult moral problems and the anxiety and guilt they can generate. Instead, we enjoy a relatively blissful and unthreatened existence. At this early stage we are also ignorant of the necessity of death, and naively presume we will live forever. Psychologically speaking, we still have access to the fruit of the tree of life.

Eventually, we learn that we and all others must die, and, with increasing experience, we inevitably "fall" away from the innocence of earliest childhood (certainly by adolescence), and are "expelled" from Paradise. It is reasonable to infer that unconscious archetypal memories such as these are the source of the symbols we find in the Yahwist's creation-and-fall account.

We may now return to the question which was asked above and reply that, symbolically (or psychologically) speaking, our "first parents" did dwell at a *mythical* time in the garden of Paradise; but, *literally* speaking, there never was such a time or place.

4. Did the first parents of the human race truly commit an original sin which was some forbidden action?

Again, our answer must be "yes" and "no." Since our first parents were truly human, they certainly possessed reason and freedom of choice and had to learn to use this power responsibly (by *their* historically limited standards, not ours). It seems reasonable to surmise, therefore, that "original sin" occurred the first time one of them acted contrary to dimly developing conscience and committed some serious injustice which produced conscious guilt and shame.

This understanding of "original sin" rules out the notion that it *literally* involved eating forbidden fruit from "the tree of the knowledge of good and evil." We learned above that eating fruit from that tree had a specific symbolic meaning for both the Yahwist and the older Mesopotamian mythmaker, whose story he revised.

5. Do we inherit a condition from our first parents called original sin, which makes us guilty and deserving of eternal punishment in God's sight?

We do *not* inherit a sinful condition from our first parents because of some "original sin" they committed. There never was a time when adult humans were immune from moral failure, guilt, suffering, and death. Such problems are simply the inevitable consequences of our finite human condition which learns by trial and error and is bound by biological limits. In precritical ages, these problems could only be explained mythologically.

There was not, therefore, an occasion on which our first parents literally were subjected to these problems as punishment, and began passing them on to their children. *However,* there is an important basis in human experience for the traditional doctrine of inherited original sin. (Remember, behind every symbol there stands an experienced reality. If this were not so, we would not have searched for a symbol to illustrate it.)

The problematic condition that we all inherit from our first parents is not the mythologically construed condition of "original sin," but, rather, the *human condition.* Since we humans are finite and temporal beings, we begin as infants bound by the condition of *helplessness* and *ignorance,* and are continually subject to (ambiguous) becoming. Many years of good example and positive instruction are required before we learn to act like responsible adults by caring for others with love and commitment. Eventually, we all can and should become responsible adults.

But when adult life becomes extremely demanding, which it periodically does, we can all unconsciously remember an earlier stage in life (infancy or adolescence) when no such demands were made of us. We then can be tempted to regress to that stage in order to escape from the demands of the present. When we irresponsibly act out such unconscious desires, some form of moral failure always results, and our creative task of completing the maturation process is disrupted. For in order to say "yes" to the requirements of truth, love, and commitment, we must all learn to say "no" to the regressive tug of our self-centered infantile past.

We do, therefore, inherit a condition from our first parents which makes us prone to selfishness and sin; its origin, however is not to be found in the literally conceived "fall" of our first parents, but in the psychological makeup of a finite being whose conscious development is always subject to the possibility of tragic disruption and harmful regression.

6. If all of the foregoing is true, then why do Christians receive the sacrament of Baptism?

The sacrament of Baptism is the symbolic way in which the Christian faith community reminds itself and its new members that the gift of healing love which God assures us of through faith in Jesus can set us free from our tendency to regress to the self-centeredness in which we were born. The memory of this earlier condition and its subsequent history remain in our unconscious mind as the basis of our capacity for irresponsible regression or sin.

We can all be tempted on occasion to despair of overcoming our perverse inclinations and misdeeds, and to fear, consequently, that God might exclude us from Eternal Life. God, nevertheless, assures us through the Risen Jesus and the gift of the Spirit (i.e., God's reconciling and enabling love), that we *can* transcend the tug of our infantile past, complete the maturation process by a life of faith, love, and service, and arrive at Eternal Life. Baptism does not, therefore, literally wash away the guilt of an inherited "original sin," but assures us through archetypal symbols that we have access to the gift of God's life-imparting love which enables us to transcend the infantile incapacity for responsibility and commitment in which we were born.

God works through the faith and love of responsible parents to *begin* gracing the life of a baptized infant with the good example and instruction necessary for learning to live an authentic Christian life. Accordingly, in the case of an infant, the prayers and sacred symbols of the baptismal ceremony are primarily intended to instruct the faith of the infant's parents and to remind them (and the Christian faith community, represented by the godparents) of their obligation to raise the child in an atmosphere of faith and love. Such an atmosphere will enable the child to outgrow the original weakness and ignorance in which it was born, and predispose it to be receptive to personal faith encounter with God and his love in adulthood.

7. If the approach to the Bible's meaning recommended in this modest monograph is correct, then has not the Church been reading the Bible incorrectly for centuries?

The church's literal reading of the Bible in some past centuries was *not* incorrect, but, rather, *less* correct in some respects. A literal reading of scripture is not devoid of truth. The general meaning of the inspired biblical text is usually accessible to any sincere reader or hearer even when taken literally.

Such a literal reading, however, is unwittingly burdened with a number of naive assumptions from the past that are joined together with the correct and enduring insights present in the text. When the increasing knowledge of later ages detects and criticizes these naive assumptions, their nonliteral (and nonessential) nature should be granted, and they should be read accordingly. But all too often, the conservative tendencies of religious people prompt them to defensively cling to the comforting certainties of the past, and to resist necessary change. This mistaken resistance causes the genuine religious meaning and authority of the Bible to be compromised, and renders the word of God suspect in the eyes of many.

The unwillingness of some conservatives to relinquish the outmoded and nonessential religious ideas of the past is the result of their mistaken identification of past assumptions about God (and the world) with the reality of God. They sincerely fear that if they deny their outmoded *assumptions* about God, they will be denying *God*, and they understandably reject that possibility as intolerable. In such a situation, the absolute authority of God is mistakenly conferred upon merely relative human expressions *about* God (and the God-human relationship), which results in the subtle and insidious form of idolatry called *Bibliolatry* (idolatrous worship of the Bible).

Those who are guilty of Bibliolatry usually assume that God has *dictated* all of the words in the Bible, and that such words may be identified with God and given divine or absolute authority. But modern biblical scholarship emphatically rejects such an interpretation as oversimplified and mythological. God does not communicate words to the prophets; rather, he communicates an experience of his own mysterious reality. Under the impact of the divine self-communication, the prophets are inspired to use language in a creative new way to teach about the reality of God and the God-human relationship.

While it is true that the words spoken by the prophets are divinely inspired, it is also true that they are culturally conditioned and historically limited. This means that in the course of expressing their inspired insights about God and the God-human relationship, the prophets unconsciously include certain assumptions from their worldview which are thought to be true at the time, but which later ages, because of increased experience, will find inadequate.

When the words that God has inspired humans to write in his service are *identified* with God and given the absolute authority that belongs to God alone, the words soon become the enemy of that spiritual progress which God himself is calling forth throughout human history.

8. *If the ideas expressed in this tract are true, then why did the Council of Trent teach infallibly that Adam truly committed original sin, truly lost immortality for himself and us, truly passed on original sin to us, and that Baptism truly washes that sin away? Is not this tract anathematized by Trent?*

The reader may be assured that no one is about to be burned at the stake. A question like the one before us, though somewhat tendentious, is basically fair; it deserves an honest answer.

In past ages when the church still read the Bible in a *literal* way, all doctrinal pronouncements meant to clarify the meaning of the Bible were based on that *literal* reading. At the present stage of history, however, the church has learned that it is no longer appropriate to read the Bible in a naively literal way. It is understandable that sacred scripture was sometimes interpreted literally in the past, but such an approach may no longer be recommended in our scientifically critical age if the sacred scriptures are to retain their credibility for present and future generations.

Since the Second Vatican Council, therefore, the church has officially taught that the Bible contains culturally conditioned literary forms which must be understood in a *nonliteral* way against their proper historical background. It follows that if the church now officially teaches that we must deliteralize our reading of the *Bible* to more adequately grasp its authentic meaning, then we must also deliteralize any *official pronouncements* about the Bible's meaning made during those centuries when the Bible was still understood literally.

The same critical principles which we bring to our interpretation of the ancient biblical text must also be applied to doctrinal pronouncements made in past ages to clarify the meaning of that text. Doctrines once provided to explain and safeguard the essential meaning of sacred scripture obviously can not claim for themselves an authority greater than scripture itself, or be exempt from the standards of critical scholarship which are applied to the very word of God.

When the church declares a doctrinal pronouncement to be infallible, she is guaranteeing its essential fidelity to the word of God, but she is not binding us permanently to the culturally conditioned assumptions once used to express or explain that word. All of the words in the Bible are inspired (i.e., they were written by an author who was moved by special faith experience of God to teach in God's service), but only those inspired words which speak with enduring validity about *God* and *the God-human relationship* are truly the word of God.

Questions for Further Study

1. Is there any truth to the traditional Christian belief that Adam and Eve were our first parents?

2. Is there any truth to the traditional Christian belief that our first parents orginally enjoyed immortality and special innocence?

3. Is there any truth to the traditional Christian belief that our first parents began their existence in the garden of Eden or Paradise?

4. Is there any truth to the traditional Christian belief that our first parents committed an original sin which was somehow passed on to us?

5. Now that we know we should not take the Genesis story of the fall literally, in what sense is the Sacrament of Baptism still meaningful and necessary?

6. At our time in history, why is it dangerous to continue reading and teaching the Genesis creation and fall accounts literally?

7. How can the present Christian faith community approve of ideas that seem to contradict the official doctrine taught by the Council of Trent in the sixteenth century?